# Mala

# Mala

Selected Poems

by

Joe Zarantonello

2008

To Pam, the Constant Gardener

# G*d

Why do we have to have
a sound, a word, a name
for the ungraspable,
the unsayable,
the unknowable,
the unbelievable?

Why not just let go
of the grasping,
the saying,
the knowing,
the believing
and the naming?

Why not just
relax
and enjoy
the infinite surprise?

# Poem du Jour

It's a really simple process—I get up about
four in the morning, have a cup of coffee,
and then go to the zendo and sit.
And after sitting, I write.
Just bringing forth whatever's within.
And later, I listen to what I wrote
with the ear of the heart.

The only way I know how to "true" a poem
is by ear, and by heart.
The heart knows what's true—
and I listen with it.
And then I just whittle away everything
that isn't true.
Whatever's left on the page—is *the poem du jour*.

Then somehow, mysteriously, the poem "trues" me.

# After 35 Years

*for Pam*

Somehow I stumbled into marriage
like a blind man wanders
into a lush garden.
I was simply following the sweet
scent of the flowers—
but to my astonishment,
I found what I really longed for
in the heart of the gardener herself.

# *Vow of Love*

Despite what all the poets say,
Love is *not* a feeling.
Not an emotion.
Rather, Love's a willingness
a vow you make
to extend yourself
to promote
a growth in consciousness
for all
for another—and for yourself.

# *Why Practice?*

Most people come to practice,
whether they know it or not,
because their ass is on fire!

Suffering.

When they asked Buddha
to describe Nirvana,
all he said was:
"Not suffering!"

So, how do you end suffering?

I don't know.
You don't need to know.
All you need
is a burning desire to inquire.

# Ante Up!

How many of us are asleep
when our ship
comes in?

How many of us lose
our invitation
to the big dance
under stacks and stacks
of junk mail?

How many of us,
by choice
or by chance,
follow
the wrong god home—
and miss our star entirely?

Not me, by God, not me.
I'm going for it!
Whole hog.
Pedal to the metal.
Cash on the barrel head.

Life, at some point,
grabs you
by the short hairs
and simply says, "Ante up!"

## One Is Enough

I don't know what's melted down—
maybe it's the last vestige
of that cast iron door
you thought would cover your heart forever

But now, you are absolutely radiant
and full of life

Could it be that you're finally
in the presence of
the one you can no longer fool
about who you really are?

The one for whom
you are always and already enough

## Go Through

After 9/11
the guru
of this
cartoon
nation
challenged
us to go
shopping

Or to go
further
(why not
mars?)

Or just to
go go go
anywhere

Yet all the
while
the ancient
angels
of despair
have been
whispering
to our
seasick souls

Go deeper
go through
go all the way

To hope

# Angelus

Frost blankets the ground and bare trees
as I set out on my morning walk.
Like the beech leaves beneath my feet
the fragile dream of life from Fallujah
to Port-au-Prince is being crushed
under the military boots of occupation.
My mind (a guernica of edgy marines
smart bombs and wounded children)
is suddenly relieved by a tiny spray
of yellow asters blooming in the ditch.

## *Walking In the Light of Day*

After a retreat, we walk down the road in the sun,
out to the middle of the green fields.
Talking of many things, past and present,
old ghosts and current fears.
Looking off to the field in tears.
Thinking of past sins
and resolving to avoid new ones.
Somehow knowing
that nothing in heaven
or on earth could pull us across
the shadow line
that both of us have crossed before.
Something stronger runs in our veins now.
Something bigger and deeper than the itch for more.
There's something beautiful between us now,
that walks the open fields, in the light of day, for all to see.

# Never Volunteer

Carl Jung once said that the avoidance
of the necessary pain of living
is the root of all mental illness.

There is the pain of life, that lasts
as long as it lasts—and then is gone.
That's simply necessary suffering.

Then there is the bitching about the pain,
which can go on for decades, even
lifetimes, after the real pain is gone.

The bitching, the complaining
is voluntary suffering—and is
the drug of choice for all victims.

Life will give each of us just enough
suffering to make us saints.
We don't need to add any of our own.

## Exile the Bitch

Exile the inner bitch
to the desert
for forty days
just to see
what life would be like
without all the
complaining
about the government,
without all the
grousing
about the job,
without all the
judgment of others,
without all the
incessant
*soto voce* resistance
to reality
just being what it is—
and see how much
energy
would really be
freed up
if you ever really
gave up
bitching about it all.

## It's Up To You

Towards the end of our morning walk, Om gamboled
through the meadow and then
just rolled on his back in the new mown hay.

It was bliss-void-indivisible on display.
All this, as the forlorn beagle at the house up on the road,
who's always chained up, kept yelping in desperate protest.

And it occurred to me, that each of us has a choice.
You can either be God—
or an ego pretending to be God. It's entirely up to you.

# Cynthia's Roadside Shrine

### for Cynthia Brinkman, SSND

The weekend before the government saw fit to lock you up
for crossing the line at the School of the Americas,
the bluets were blooming in Ellington
and we kicked up our heels among them
to the heartbeat of Spring
and the eternal downbeat of the Godfather of Soul

Two weeks later, as I was walking down the road in the hollow,
lost in wonder at the green revolution about to burst forth,
I happened upon an explosion of bluets by the roadside.
I stopped and smiled and thought of you
in some dark place, held as a prisoner of conscience
by the most powerful government in the world
who is quite rightly afraid of such a gentle Quaker Lady

I breathed in the freshness of the morning air,
of the electric green tulip poplar leaves just now unfurling,
of red bud and red clover, of the creek running wild with rain.
I breathed it all in for you, behind bars in Pekin, and for the man
in the White House—dreaming of a freedom as great as yours.

# *Ordinary Time*

Up in the monastery balcony,
Nashville Mona Lisa
sits serene in sapphire blouse,
tight black jeans,
& yellow cowboy boots—
just soaking up the silence.
Melting into afternoon
sunlight
streaming
through blue stained glass.
No monks, no chant
& nothing
special—
just a simple grace note,
just ordinary time
at the Abbey of Gethsemani.

# New Grammar

God
The Way It Is
The Dharma
The Kingdom of Heaven
Enlightenment & Endarkenment
& Absolutely Everything
In-Between
Is Simply
A Verb

# You Bet Your Life

Are you betting your life
that once you achieve
financial security, then
you will be able spend
the rest of your life
doing what really matters?

How many people do you know
who have actually won that bet?

Instead, if you are willing
to tolerate the hardships
that flow from doing
what matters most right now,
you can bet your life
on a game that you can't lose.

# Wound Healing Wound

It rained and rained
    and rained last spring
        and our pond overflowed

Slashing deep gashes
    in the land
        which bled blue clay

And stone. This fall
    we hauled wheelbarrow
        after wheelbarrow

Of those bloody stones
    to fill the ruts
        in our road.

Season after season,
    rending and mending,
        wound healing wound

All on the rough road to wholeness.

## Facing the Great Emptiness

The death of a mother, a father, a child or a loved one
brings us into contact with a great emptiness.
You can resist the emptiness through distraction,
addition or sedation—or you can accept the invitation
to journey deeper into the emptiness.
The moments of great emptiness that life gives us all
are thresholds that lead to total transformation.
Life will always give you the choice, thank goodness,
to say "no" to resistance—and "yes" to everything else.

# Why Are You Unhappy?
## after listening to a lecture by Bob Thurman

Why are you unhappy? Why can't you enter the Gateless Gate
of Bliss—which is always open, with no hinges to rust?
Both questions have the same answer—
"Because—because everything that you think,
and all that you do,
is for yourself—and there isn't one."

Oh sure, there is this confused, angst-ridden, uptight
fictional self that we are all truly convinced is really really us!
But is this a self worth having? Is this a self worth maintaining?
Make no mistake about it, it takes all the energy we can muster
to just maintain this virtual suffering that we call our "self."

When the Roman soldiers entered the Holy of Holies
on the day they began to destroy the Temple—
they found a completely empty room.
Not being trained in Buddhist dialectics, however,
they missed the point entirely.

And we all know what became of Rome and the Empire.

# The Dead of Winter

All the ponds are frozen. The pumps unplugged
and stored in the barn. All the hoses
removed from the spigots.

At my writing desk, I listen as the oak, beech
and maple bow low under a cloak of ice.
Their limbs crack in the night like rifle fire.

e.e. cummings is taped to my study window—

*I'd rather learn from one bird how to sing*
*than teach ten thousand stars not to*
*dance.*

And I wonder, do I still believe that?

My fingers used to emit sparks of fire
with expectation of my future labors.
Has that blaze become, at last,
cold ash?

It's the dead of winter. It's that time of year
we are all called to ask: What has died inside?
And what is just wintering over?

# *That Swing*

The inevitable question:
"And what do you do?"

Oh, I help people
build swings.

You help people
build swings?

Yeah, exactly. I help folks
build swings
on the front porch
of their souls.

Help them create a space
where they can
sip lemonade,
and waste some time,
everyday, with God.

Really? Really.

To paraphrase the Duke:
You don't mean a thing
If you ain't got that swing!

# Like Bartimaeus

In his quiet, fierce way, the Dutch Zen master
asked forty of us, one day, before we sat—
"What do you really want?"

"I don't mean your whole Christmas list—
just tell me the one thing
that is your heart's deepest desire."

We are all blind beggars, just like Bartimaeus,
until we've sat and pondered the question
in the deep silence of the heart—

*What is the one thing that my soul longs for?*

## Sit, Write, Live

I have absolutely nothing against exotic travel to foreign lands.
And I certainly have no bone to pick with
spending four months eating in Italy,
praying in an ashram in India,
or having a tempestuous love affair in Bali—
although my wife might have a bone to pick with that last one.

Traveling across the ocean blue might work quite well for you—
but for me, it's all about exploring the true nature
of reality—right here, right now.
No passport, itinerary or frequent-flier miles necessary!

An old Chinese Zen Master put it this way—
*Magical power, marvelous action!*
*Chopping wood, carrying water....*
But for me, it's always been even simpler—"Sit, Write, Live."

## Glancing Up I Saw You

Glancing up from my writing, I saw you
reclining on your cushion,
Jewish prayer shawl
draped across your shoulders
like a blessing at dawn—
words streaming out of your pen
like a river running through the desert.

The glance caught a faint smile on your face.
Not the smile of the earnest schoolgirl
who had finally solved the fucking equation!
But rather, the smile of a ransomed queen,
recently returned from foreign lands—
bemused and at ease with her own words
flowing like golden honey from the golden comb.

## Naked Christians for Peace

Imagine Naked Christians for Peace, half-a-million strong,
gathering on The National Mall. Men and women. Old and young.
Gay and straight. White, black, brown and yellow. Saints
and sinners. All naked and shining like the sun.

Imagine a sea of naked Christians from the Lincoln Memorial
all the way to the Houses of Congress. Can you just imagine
a tidal wave of naked Christians turning the other cheek,
toward the White House, for peace?

# Write It All Down

*for William Stafford*

Longest night of the year and it's
well below zero. Four days before
Christmas. Satellites clotted
with images of elves, reindeer
and shopping—as the blood of the
poor flows into the mud of Haiti,
Darfur, Cleveland and Chiapas.

"You don't have to prove anything,"
you wrote on the day you died.
"Just be ready for what God sends."
And write it all down "the way it is."
You made it all sound so easy. Just
follow the light wherever it leads—
even into the shadows.

# The Fall

The music
stops
and the dance
with God is over,
the moment
I say,
"I don't want
to dance that way."

Or—"It would be
better
this way."

All the music
stops.
And the dance
with God is over,
the moment
I think,
"I should be
the one who leads."

# The Three Jewels

What are the rarest commodities
in the world today?
Gold, diamonds or uranium?
No, the three jewels of great price
in the 21st Century are
silence, stillness and simplicity.

# Sitathon

Why would consenting adults of sound mind
choose to sit in meditation nine times a day
for five days straight in almost total silence?

Well, it's really quite simple.

To learn how to rest.
To drop veil after veil after veil.
To imagine a life that's truly worth living.
And to gain the energy and courage to live it.

# Super 8

*pleasure*
*pain*

*gain*
*loss*

*praise*
*blame*

*fame*
*disgrace*

slow
down

the old
projector

and we
can see

celluloid
reality

flicker
flicker

into
illusion

## Flower Sutra

being present to
everything

and resisting
nothing

allows the bud
of wisdom

to flower
naturally

and to release
effortlessly

the balm
of compassion

that is meant
to heal the world

# Being World Peace
### on the second anniversary of the Iraq War

Hundreds of thousands in Washington and millions worldwide
will be marching today for peace—as I sit here in the zendo
with three others, on our meditation cushions, in the silence.

I am more convinced than ever that world peace will remain elusive
until we establish a platform of inner peace in individuals.
There can be no way to peace—if peace itself is really the way.

The wars and conflicts that we see in the world are simply
manifestations of the wars and conflicts that rage
in our own heart of hearts.

Human confusion is powerful, and power is confusing.
The confusion in the heart of the world
is greater than ever.

But the clarity in some human hearts is also greater than ever—
and is spreading across the planet
at the speed of light.

So things are getting better and worse at the same time.
When and where these two energies meet—
no telling what will happen!

But in the meantime, have no illusions about changing others,
or ending the world's confusion once and for all.
Your mission is, simply—not to let the confusion change you!

For the Buddha and Jesus showed us time and time again
that bringing forth your true self into this world
is how you can be the peace that surpasses all understanding.

# Hokey Pokey

You make Awareness the master
And thinking the servant

You make Now primary
And time secondary

You make Being your purpose
And doing flows from it

This is how you turn yourself around
And that's *really* what it's all about

# Alternative Energy

I always feel like I'm plugged into a 220-volt socket
when I give a retreat at a convent or motherhouse.
I'm not exactly sure why.

Well, for one thing, it's probably the prayer.
Women have been praying here together
for over a hundred years.

But also, just maybe, it's the accumulation
of all that poised and beautiful
virginal energy.

If you're gonna walk the celibate road with joy,
you've got to have skillful training
in how to transform all that heat into light.

Somehow, great spiritual women like Catherine of Siena,
Teresa of Avila, Hildegard of Bingen, Julian of Norwich,
Mother Seton, Mother Teresa

And countless other women, so many of them unknown,
have mastered this sexual alchemy—and have learned
how to transform the big bang into Love.

Well, to be deadly honest—
I never expected to be writing a poem
about harnessing the sexual energy of nuns!

But hey, why not get in on the ground floor now—
and invest in your nearest motherhouse
before Exxon-Mobil gets wind of it!

Like fossil fuels, nuns are an extremely precious resource.
But unlike oil or coal, nuns are perpetually renewable!
And let us pray to God—that they always will be.

*Mount St. Joseph, Ohio*
*November 2006*

# Sharpen Your Mind

Sharpen your mind like a fine, steel knife.
Each and every morning—sit and write,
sit and write each and every day.
Don't worry about cutting yourself—
clean wounds heal the quickest.
Besides, it's the dull knife that'll kill you.

# In Good Company

You prayed and prayed and prayed until
your knees ached
and your knuckles turned white
and still you didn't get what you wanted.
And now you feel frightened and angry.

Were my prayers not good enough?
Was God just not persuaded?
Maybe God had other plans.
Or maybe God just didn't give a damn.
Or just maybe there is no God
and this is all just a random crap shoot!

All these thoughts ran through the mind
of Mary at the foot of the cross.
Dear one, you are in good company
as you ponder all of this
in the deep, deep silence of your heart.

# How Old Are You Anyway?

*for Gregory Lambing, OCSO*

Walking up the dirt road to the Hermitage, I was
having trouble keeping up with the monk.

Out of breath, I paused and called to him—
"How old *are* you, anyway?"

He paused, and turned toward me grinning—
"Do you mean my body or my soul?"

I laughed and took the bait, "Your soul?
How can a soul age?"

"Oh, that's easy," he said, "Every moment spent
in presence ages and ripens your soul."

We walked on around the bend in the red clay road
and up to Merton's cinderblock hideaway.

We sat in silence on the front porch for an hour
just listening to the wind in the trees.

# The Enneagram of Suffering

The One: I deserve everything I get. Got a hairshirt?

The Two: Let me help you with your suffering.

The Three: Suffering? I don't have time for suffering!

The Four: Nobody knows the suffering I know....

The Five: I'd rather burn in hell than let go of my suffering!

The Six: I'm not sure — What is suffering, anyway?

The Seven: Which way to the luau?

The Eight: Suffering!?! I'll give you suffering!!!

The Nine: ZZZZZZ....

# On The Road

Kerouac had it right: we are all on the road,
all of us heading back home. The problem is
we take temporary lodging along the way,
and when we wake up the next morning—
we've totally forgotten where it was
that we were headed.

And we think the flop house we're in is home.

Whether it's a relationship, your job, your house,
your persona or this incarnation—
be grateful for all of them.
But always remember, that all of them
are no more, or less, than a cheap motel
along the great blue highway heading home.

# Anyone Can Find It

The heat pump switches off, and it is so quiet you can hear
the lady bugs crawl across the ceiling.
Downstairs, with the push of a button, the whole
world would come roaring out of my Macintosh.
But that's for later. The early morning is for this.

Nowhere to go, nothing to do. Just listening to presence.
It tends to ripen things, you know. And then something
eventually moves out of the shadows and into the light,
to meet and to be met. How do others manage to go on living
without this kind of meeting? I wonder.

And the funny thing is, anyone can find it!
As long as you are willing to wake up before other people.

# E-mail from God

You keep obsessing about
what you haven't yet
become....

And I keep on praising
what you already
are.

For heaven's sake,
who told you
that you were naked?

Get back to me on this, OK?

# Communion

I remember a monastic "Late Show,"
after *Compline* at the Abbey,
when Fr. Matthew was raving on
like John Donne all about
the communion of saints
and how we'd all been prayed
through countless moments
by all souls living and dead—
when a woman spoke up
(the only time I ever witnessed
one of Matthew's jazz improvs
being interrupted) and she said,
matter-of-factly, "Excuse me,
Father, but I'm a Baptist—
and we don't believe you can,
or should, pray for the dead.
Or that the dead pray for you."
Kelty smiled, wiped his brow,
and replied kindly, "Madam,
that may be so, but I couldn't
even conceive of living
in a universe that impoverished!"

# Haiti Again

Why do I return to Haiti again and again?
Well, it's simply to plant a tiny seed
of Presence—and then water it
with great Openness.

When, how or if ever this seed bears fruit
(in the lives of a few Haitians, or
in my own life) is not my concern.
That's entirely in the hands of the Spirit.

# Crossing the Massacre River

I am writing this poem right now for all the Haitian layabouts
at the Dajabon bridge. For all of you who carried our luggage
across the Massacre River on your heads.

I am writing this poem for all the old, ragged desperadoes
who helped us ford the river and climb the steep bank
to safety and the Dominican Republic.

I am writing this poem for the poorest of the poor who were
forced back into that river at gunpoint—with sharpened
sticks and curses hurled by the Dominican soldiers.

And I know I can remain sane—only, if I refuse to forget you:
wading calf-deep in a river still crimson with memories.
Every one of you, an outlaw and a saint.

*8 February 2006*

N.B.: *In 1937, the Dominican dictator Trujillo slaughtered hundreds of
Haitian cane cutters and then dumped them into the Massacre River.
They say the river ran red with blood for days.*

# Original Spin

When did we lose confidence in our basic goodness?
Was it in some mystical garden?
Was it due to Original Sin?
Or does it happen, inexplicably, in each moment?
Does it happen when we feel the background humming
with anxiety about our own inner light?
When we feel a sense of general inadequacy
that darkens everything we do?
Somehow we have become afraid of our own light.
Somehow we have become deeply afraid of feeling that fear.
And so all that we think, say and do spins a cocoon to protect us—
but in the process, obscures what we are all so madly searching for.

# Worst-Case Scenario

Perhaps death is not the worst-case scenario?
And if it isn't—then you might ask illness, hunger,
financial insecurity and failure: "Where is thy sting?"
But if death is not the worst of evils—then what is?
Well, you could ask me if what I have lived is *my* life.

# Getting the Knack of It

Yes, at last, I am getting the knack of sitting meditation!
The fact that I have been sitting for 34 years now,
and that I feel that I am just now "getting the knack of it"—
either attests to the fact that I am some sort of spiritual retard;
or perhaps, that simply sitting in this present moment
is one of the subtlest art forms ever attempted by human beings.

# *Virus*

4:28 A.M. and I am shivering and sweating through my clothes.
Box of Nice and Soft tissue at my elbow,
pumped full of chamomile tea and Coricidan.
Three days since I've sat.
I can't remember ever missing two days in a row
ever.

It takes all my energy and focus just to get out of bed and pee.
So lots of lying in the bed
in malarial dream states of consciousness.

At first it was fear that I felt, "Shit, what is this bug?
Maybe it'll turn into pneumonia!"
Then I began to do Tonglen. Good ole Tonglen.

At first working with my own fear, and then moving on to work
with all the people on the planet
lying sick right now
with no roof over their head and no hope of cure.

And I well up with gratitude that I have a house, and a bed,
and meds—and I use this gratitude to power whatever
healing I can send out to all the poor of this world.
To the young Haitian girl lying in bed with AIDs.
To the people on the gulf coast still without homes.
To all the needy and forsaken.

Perhaps gratitude is an even stronger virus than influenza.
Let us pray for a pandemic of gratefulness.
Let us pray.

## Limerick of Liberation

I once knew a romantic junkie
who jumped from man to man like a monkey;
but when she found Zen,
she lost her craving for men—
and now she's enlightened and spunky!

## Sext Before Dinner

The Abbey bells peel like thunder
as Kelty careens around the corner
into choir on his chic, beige
monastic go-cart.
He sits parked, at the end
of the choir stalls,
hunched forward a bit, and dozing—
as he waits for the chanting to begin.
Not a bad life, at 90, to have
*Sext* before dinner and *None* after.

*N.B.: Sext and None—the sixth and ninth*
*"hours" of the Divine Office.*

# The New Math

If the Universe is a friendly place,
as every mystic contends—
then why is its favorite game
takeaway?

Why does Life take away
this and that,
family and friends,
our dreams and even our health?

Who knows! But just maybe this
spirituality of subtraction
is the only kind of equation
that the ego can never solve.

Maybe loss after loss after loss
is the only way
that our Life ever really
adds up.

This mystic calculus of the heart,
which is as old as the soul itself—
will always be called
The New Math.

# Graceful

In one shining moment
in some lifetime
it will dawn on you

Just as it dawned
for Merton
on that street corner

It will dawn on you
that time and space
are full of grace

That the light shines
not upon
each one of us

But from within
each
one of us

From the largest galaxy
to the smallest quark
graceful, graceful

Graceful

# Cut It Out

A moment here
spent
judging God.

A moment there
spent
judging others.

Eternity spent
forever
judging yourself.

There is
no such thing
as just a little cancer.

So cut it out.
For heaven's sake,
cut it out—and forgive.

# *Words Matter*

All the great ancient traditions remind us
that words matter

Buddha found that words
could conceal reality
so he dropped them all—
as he plunged into the silence
of deep meditation

Jesus lived and died to show us
that words from the soul of a poet
could reveal reality as well—
and as he breathed his last
the veil in the temple was rent

Buddha and Jesus—
word into silence and silence into word

# *Meditation*

In a single breath

Return

Release

Relax

And Rest

Rest in the Mind

That neither Seeks nor Grasps

# Contemplation

After the mud has settled

Uncap the pen
And go

And don't stop
Writing

Until you see
Deeply

Deeply into the heart
Of things

Or until the fat lady sings

# Living With Impermanence

A recent show on the Discovery Channel called
"Living with Cancer"
really bowled me over.
I was thunderstruck by the luminous energy
that some of the cancer survivors emitted.
They were so alive!
As one of them explained,
"We have lots of time to think about death."

This morning on my walk down the road
it occurred to me—
"Hell, I'm 'Living with Impermanence!'"
I am every bit as "terminal" as anyone who has
stage-four cancer.
The difference is: they know it. And the rest of us do not.
We take walks under the gorgeous morning sky
and we're oblivious.
We never ever feel the absolute miracle of the gravel
beneath our feet.

Well, this morning I gazed up at the clouds,
and I wiggled my toes—
and I realized the utter impermanence of all of it.
And everything around me, I mean everything—
became alive and luminous.

# The Hamster Wheel

Work to spend
Work to spend
Work to spend

And then work some more
So you can spend some more

Work to spend
Work to spend
Work to spend

Until the consumer is finally
Consumed in the act of consumption

Work to spend
Work to spend
Work to spend

Until your precious soul is completely spent

# At the Tomb of the Unknown Soldier

Robot soldier. 21 steps. 21 seconds. Turn.
Pause for 21 seconds.
Repeat.

Cult of the gun.
Cult of meaningless precision.
Cult of war.

Military Kabuki.
5 minutes inspecting the rifle with white-gloved hands.
Patent leather shoes. Clicking heels. Cult of the automatic.

"Kinda hypnotic, ain't it..."
one of the chaperones muses.
Exactly.

So many white crosses.
Hillside after hillside of white crosses.
"When you awaken,
you will remember nothing," the Hypnotist whispers.

*Memorial Day 2006*

## Lower Your Standards

To lower your standards
in times of king and castle meant
to lower your flag.
Raising your standard
was the rallying cry for war,
a call to arms.
So lowering your standards is a kind of
unilateral declaration of peace.
No war on the present moment.

Lower your standards completely—
and see what happens to your life.
See what happens when you declare peace
in this moment.
Lower your standards,
put down your weapons,
and enter each moment unarmed, open.

Surrender meant to give the land you leased
back to the lord
who owned it originally.
None of us owns
the present moment, we just lease it.
To surrender means to give each moment
back to the Lord,
to lower our standards completely,
and to just love what is.

Why is that so hard?
Why is it so hard to lower our standards,

collect all the swords,
beat them into plowshares, and end all this madness?

Why is it so hard to get on with the real work
of being human?
The work of living each moment
"on earth as it is in heaven?"
Lower your standards completely,
and dance—as the Gates of Eden swing.

## The Shortest Distance

The shortest distance between two points
is not a straight line.
For that matter,
there is no such thing as two points.
There is no such thing as Point B.
There is only Point A—only here, only now.
And the shortest distance between
here and now
is simply a graceful bow to just this moment.

# *Slow Hand*

"Once you get a laptop, you'll forget how to write with a pen."

"You'll be able to write twice as much, twice as fast!"

The hype goes on and on. But I'm not impressed.

One of the things I like most about writing by hand

        is that it slows me down.

Handwriting gives my soul some time—time to listen, and time

to catch up, to catch up with this bullet-train that some call a life.

# Before It's Too Late

Take a break from thinking all the time
and for once—really see a flower

Take a break from thinking so much
and just listen to the music
rain makes
falling through the poplar trees

Take a mini-holiday from thought
and eat a fruit salad
out on the back porch
and take the time to taste the fruit

Strike a huge blow against the Empire
and just spend an hour or two
relaxing and musing
on whatever tickles your fancy

Before it's too late, find your own way—
your own way of looking at things

# The Guns at Fort Knox
### *after three years of "Shock and Awe"*

The big guns at Fort Knox are booming—shaking, rattling
and rolling across forty miles of Kentucky knobs
and right into this quiet zendo. The same shock waves
rattled the windows in Merton's hermitage 40 years ago.

I used to feel: "How ironic: as we sit down to meditate,
they begin unleashing the big guns—boom,
booming and shaking the entire house as if
a giant was marching straight through the Hollow."

But now it no longer seems ironic—but perfect.
For in fact, we sit here because they train for death there.
No longer sitting against these boys, and all their
dangerous toys. No, now I sit with them.

As I sit with my own fear, despair and aggression—
and know that it is no different from theirs.
No different from what motivates the Masters of War
at the Pentagon, or at Lockheed or Los Alamos.

Yes, I sit with all of them—and because of them.
Dying to know, in the marrow of my soul—
if there's a great peace to be found
even beneath the sound of the guns at Fort Knox.

*20 March 2006*

## Macho Dilemma

Well, if you can't hunt it, kill it
or skin it. And if you can't
eat it, fight it or fuck it—
What in the hell can you do with it?

# *Desperadoes*

Taking the time to get a manicure, pedicure,
facial, sauna or massage—
these are all things
that you would do at a spa
to celebrate and revitalize your body.

The body is a great gift and ought to be
treated with gratitude and reverence.
But what have you done lately
to celebrate and revitalize your soul?

Our souls are literally "desperadoes,"
desperate for one thing
and one thing only—ripening.
Good and bad, pleasure or pain—
they don't matter at all to our souls.
Our souls know, somehow, that ripeness is all.

# The Soul Child

Beneath all the judgment
lies the anger
and the shame
and the need for control

And quite safely beneath
all these veils
of protective gauze
lies the Soul Child—

So vulnerable, so innocent,
so completely blissful—
as it waits patiently,
ultimately, to be discovered.

# Of Moths and Monks

Wal-Mart Zen monks look like they're sitting
motionless
on their cushions—
but really, most are forever
fluttering
around the memory
of that brief flash of enlightenment,
they experienced, sometime, in the past.

Wal-Mart monks are a lot like moths—
compulsively driven toward the light.
Real Zen monks sit with eyes, ears, nose,
mouth and hearts wide-open—
right in the middle of the deep,
muddy, raging river of this moment.
Smack dab in the muddle
of all their funky fears, anger and desire.

Which will you choose to be—moth or monk?

## Hardtack

On the surface of things
you feel dark and lonely
and isolated.

You feel like you are
blazing a trail
to nowhere.

You feel like turning around
retracing your steps
and admitting defeat.

But then, miraculously,
the soul urges you to
"Press on! Keep exploring!"

And if you do indeed press on,
confidence and gratitude
will well up

from some deep down spring
just when you feel like
you're most empty.

This confidence and gratitude
is the basic hardtack
of all spiritual explorers.

# Ground Zero

For a few terribly beautiful days following 9/11—
New York City
became the heart of the world.

For a brief, fragile moment in time,
the business of America
was no longer just business.

In the absolute groundlessness that followed
the collapse of what the world thought
was so permanent—

In the place that everybody called Ground Zero,
the mind of America stopped for awhile—
and our hearts knew instantly

That kindness was the only thing that really mattered.

# Humiliation Cocktail

1 Shot of Pride
1 Shot of Vanity
1 Shot of Desire

Shaken not stirred, and served over crushed
expectations—with a twist of revenge.

# *Mind*

If you could
just

let it be

the jungle
would

spontaneously

become
a garden

without
destroying

a single flower

## The Human Path

From Edvard Munch's "The Scream"
to Leonardo's "Mona Lisa"

From the clenched fist
to the open hand

From strategy
to let it be

From perpetual warfare
to eternal peace

This is the human path
from compulsion to contemplation

## We Shall See

Isn't the truth—rather than sex or a shot glass—
the gateway to intimacy? We shall see.

"It's all so unfamiliar," he whispered,
as he kept tiptoeing across the threshold
between this life and the next.

The doorway—Death—though strange,
has no width. So how can it sting?

In the end, what anybody thinks of you,
or what you think of them—
isn't all that important. Just brain farts.

But your true self, your soul—what about that?
We shall see, dear one, we shall see.

# Equanimity

Sometimes shit happens. Sometimes joy happens.
And sometimes, life just seems so utterly bland.
Nobody can control all the causes and conditions
underlying what arises in this moment.
So, no matter what's happening right now:
whether it's pleasant, unpleasant or neutral—
just be as present, as open, and as fluid as you can.

# *Transit*

buddha was
buddha is
buddha does

obscuration
realization
manifestation

insane asylum
zendo
the buddhaverse

# Confessions of a Merton Catholic

Eying my Tibetan wrist-mala she asked,
"Are you a Roman Catholic?"
"Oh no," I responded proudly, "I'm a Merton Catholic."

"A Merton Catholic—what's that?"

"Well, presence and openness are the primary sacraments.
And our theology amounts to nothing more than
unconditional friendliness
and respect for all of the world's great religions—
though we claim none of them exclusively as our own."

"Merton believed that?" she asked. "Hell no," I said. "He lived it!"

# The Great Harvest

When we sit with an emotion in zazen
    facing it
    feeling it
    & flowing through it

then the personal and self-centered
    thoughts
    separate out

and we're left with pure energy
    which can be used
    for whatever
    life needs

To harvest the energy of emotion
    on a regular basis
    in the service of compassion

is what could be called "enlightenment"

# Stages of Enlightenment

I
aluminum foil
wrapped around
nothing at all

II
wax paper
wrapped around
nothing at all

III
saran wrap
wrapped around
nothing at all

IV
nothing at all
wrapped around
everything

# Big Mind

When you stir a teaspoon of salt
into a glass of water
it becomes undrinkable.

But when you stir that same
teaspoon of salt
into Lake Superior
it has no effect whatsoever.

So it is with the mind.

A teaspoon of pain or conflict
will upset the small mind.
But the same pain or conflict
will not disturb the Big Mind.

When your mind becomes bigger
you will actually feel
more pain—
but it will bother you less.

Meditation unveils Big Mind.

## Don't Make Decisions

Who has the deep trust and patience
To wait
For the Muddy Water
To become crystal clear?

Who can simply give up making
Decisions
In favor of
Listening for them?

And who can finally let
Compassion
Flow naturally
From their own Heart of Hearts?

The Wise.
The Buddhas.
All the Saints and Mystics.
And even you, dear friend, even you.

# Across Every Threshold

I'm not sure my teenage daughter has ever heard
of carrying the bride across the threshold.

Last night I saw a movie set in East Germany
just before the Berlin Wall fell.
A writer hid his typewriter beneath a floorboard
in the doorway between two rooms.

The mystical sufis call their aspirants "dervishes."
It means, literally, "a thresholder."
Some of them "whirl about" to help them
cross the threshold from this world to the next.

I remember carrying a pillow to our first Lamaze class.
We were 3 weeks late in starting
and Aran came early.
I was speed-reading the book in between contractions.
When this tsunami of a contraction left us both
out of breath and shaken,
I remember reading: "You have now entered 'transition.'"

For the Tibetans, death is like a sacred borderline that
doesn't separate two countries—
but rather connects them—a kind of
widthless check point where your passport is always valid.

I know a remarkable woman who is living with cancer.
She has vowed to walk through every doorway,
to enter every room, and every moment, mindfully.
Whether walking into the bathroom from the kitchen,

or walking through death into the great mystery—
she's vowed to simply carry herself across every threshold.

# On the Sea of Galilee

*for Hans Koenen Roshi, SJ*

Halfway through a five-day Zen sesshin.
Five hours a day of sitting in silence,
and literally, facing our shadows
on a blank, white wall. Legs and backsides
scream "No!"—as beyond all logic,
a few of us bow to the center of the zendo,
to get in "an extra sit" before bedtime.

According to the Gospels, Jesus never really
walked on water—he walked "on the sea."
For the Jews, the sea was a symbol of chaos.
So to say that Jesus "walked on the sea"—
was like claiming that he walked across chaos,
and even death itself, to reach the other side.

Some sit on chairs, some kneel on benches,
and some sit on cushions called zafus.
In the on-line catalogue, the cushion that
I sit on is called The Tibetan Mountain Seat.
But I have nicknamed it—"The Sea of Galilee."

## The Body Is the Prayer
### for Truus Sijm, OP

Whether he walked on water or not,
Jesus was surely the greatest poet
to have ever set foot on earth.

The way he walked, the way he ate,
the way he spoke, the way he healed
(the feet, the hands, the tongues,
the eyes, the hearts and minds)
the very way he lived
always embodied The Holy One.

To embody The Holy One
in the way we sit, in the way we walk,
in the way we bow, in the way we breathe—

To embody The Holy One in the poetry
of flesh and blood—that is why we're here.

# *No Way*

Jesus could walk upon
the sea
because he was light

and even to this day
that clear light
dances
on the wine-dark sea

But there is
no way
of becoming that light

simply because
you
already are
the way and the light

# Buddhist Calculus

Suffering equals Pain plus Resistance.
Healing equals Pain plus Willingness.

The path of human being
is quite difficult.

Suffering is optional.

# *Winning the War*

Well, all the talking heads and pundits agree:
"Losing this war is not an option."
But at some point, hopefully
people will begin to wonder,
"Who could win this awful war?"
Not the American people.
Not the Iraqi people.
True, all the CEOs at Halliburton,
Blackwater, Exxon-Mobil,
the weapons makers
and all the merchants of terror—
they are celebrating
and laughing all the way to the bank.
But as Jesus once warned—
Does it really profit a man
to gain the whole world
if he loses his soul in the bargain?
For as the Buddha discovered—
In war all sides, inevitably, lose.
Beating the Kaiser gave us Hitler.
Beating Hitler gave us Stalin.
Beating the Russians gave us Osama.
And beating Osama?
Who will that give us?
Undoubtedly, the only way
to really "win a war"—is to end it.
End it with a simple Declaration of Peace.

# Zen Blackjack

Zen monks look forward to afternoon sitting about as much as
normal folks look forward to having root canal work done.
Your ass and legs ache, your lunch is only half-digested,
and you are either on the nod or thinking of jumping ship entirely.
That's when the roshi's assistant prowls the zendo
with a long, flat zen yardstick looking at you with a blank stare,
like a blackjack dealer in Vegas, and if you bow as he walks past,
that's a sign saying "Hit me!"—and he whacks you two times,
once on either side of the spine, after which you bow again
in a gesture of thanks. And the crazy thing is: you kinda like it!

# Going Home

*after a retreat*

It has nothing to do with
stripping and remaking
the bed.

It has nothing to do with
packing your suitcase
and retracing your steps.

And it has absolutely nothing
to do with getting back
to so-called "reality."

On the other hand, it has
everything to do
with finding the thread

And simply following it—
out of the cold, lonely
labyrinth of the mind

# Trappist Zen

Just sit yourself down somewhere quiet.
Sit like you're a king or a queen.
Sit poised and relaxed.

Just breathe.
Breathe into the heartspace.
Breathe out all self-centered thoughts.

And then, just listen.
Listen with the ear of the heart.
Listen and just experience life as it is.

Again and again, just return
To this practice of Trappist Zen—
Just sitting, breathing and listening.

# The Six O'Clock Saint

A six o'clock saint walks straight,
talks straight,
and walks the talk straight.

A six o'clock saint always sits straight
like the hands on a clock—
dancing in eternity
by aligning the spine with gravity.

But most of all, a six o'clock saint
loves sipping the whiskey
of just this moment—
straight, no chaser,
in the dimly lit tavern that some
have come to call Total Transformation.

# After Skeletons

It has been a hellish two weeks since you died.

Lobsters cross the ocean floor of my soul,
claws dripping with stomach lining,
scuttling from wasteland to wasteland.
Should I eat a peach?
Should I go back and teach?
What's the point ? We all end up the same—
with a bow tie and a cold ass. Six feet under.

Lying flat on my back, on the floor of my study,
next to the pink plastic waste basket
brimming with crumpled abortions in looseleaf—
a quiver filled with broken arrows.
Coffee didn't help. Writing didn't help.
Flat on my back, and clearly beyond help,
I can finally hear the wisdom in the wind
and blowing rain: "If it's broke, don't fix it."

It's been raining since the day you died,
yet this lake of grief is dry as dust.
When you were alive,
I'd go for days without thinking of you.
Now, you are in my thoughts every day.
Still, this vast forsaken lake is empty,
empty of everything but the shadow
of a question that circles and circles
like some huge bird of prey crying—
"Empty of what? Empty, empty—of what?"

Winds of anguish blow through the house.
Skeletons wave like wheat as they drift
from room to empty room.
Yet, in the silence of meditation,
breathing the very air in your dark coffin,
flesh finally begins to form on these bones,
and once again, in the stillness, I can dance.

# One Helluva Dream
### The night before The State of the Union Speech

I have a dream that the late James Brown
is cartwheeling
through the bardo,
between this life and the next,
and for no particular reason
reincarnates as George Bush
while he's taking his afternoon nap.

And let me tell you, I am so totally
on the edge of my seat—
just waiting
for the Godfather of Soul
to address the State of the Union!

I mean, will Dubya be wearing his cape?
Will Laura and Condi be shimmering
in red satin, singing back-up?
Will Cheney and the Joint Chiefs
boogaloo through the halls of Congress
proclaiming out loud—
  "I'm black and I'm proud!"?

I don't know.
But I do have a dream—and it feels good!

# What Gets Me Out of Bed Most Days

Today like every other day I woke up and eyed the clock—
it was 3:28. Somehow, it's always harder to get up
and practice in Fall. Perhaps, it's that all of nature
is bedding down for the winter? I don't know.
But I do know this: it matters.
In fact, it might be the only thing that really does matter.

When it's really tough going, and the warmth and comfort
of the blankets whisper their oh-so-sweet siren song—
I think of all my dharma pals, lying there, eying the clock.
Or what's worse, hitting the snooze button and thinking,
"Oh hell, does it really matter?"

Well folks, I'm here to say that it does, indeed, matter
whether you crawl out of bed and practice—or go back to sleep.
Willingness is nearly everything on the spiritual path.
Willingness—and interdependence.
You see, none of us sits alone. And none of us wakes up alone.
Your sitting helps the whole world.
And your waking up this morning, helps the whole world wake up.

Every morning, every effort, matters.
And knowing, that we're all in this together,
and helping each other, forever—is what gets me out of bed on
days like this.

# *Homily*

I often sit and listen to the giant sycamore near the stream in
the garden
behind the retreat house at Gethsemani. Its mammoth limbs
like polished ivory, bespeckled here and there
with archipelagos of gray bark. Majestic in leafless vestments
it proclaims the resurrection
with a silence
far deeper
than any homily

# Hell In Japanese

A Zen Master once told me
that "Hell," in Japanese,
is a character
that means "no space"

Think about that all you want.

And then one day,
when you're finally ready,
the tightly-clenched fist of thought
will just open like a beautiful flower

# Oddball Manifesto

Well, the psychiatrists have done it again!
They have come up with a new diagnosis.
They have come up with a new disorder:
O.D.D.—Oppositional Defiance Disorder.

As if it would be disordered, or even
remotely sick, to  be opposed to the rape
of the planet by the corporate lunatics
who run most of the world's governments!

No! Support all those who oppose and defy
the Wal-Martization of your town and mine.
Support the troops all over the planet—from
the streets of Seattle to the fields of Chiapas.

Support the indigenous people all over the world
who are defying the WTO and refusing to cede
the land of their ancestors to Cargill and Conagra.
Support *these* troops with your yellow ribbons!

Oddballs of the World—it's time to unite!
We have only our chains, and prozac, to lose.
Indeed, the whole planet has just begun to fight.
And to rage, rage against the dying of the light!

# I.E.D.

Just like snagging a trip-wire
one casual comment
can trigger an explosion
of ancient negative emotions

One minute a pleasant stroll,
and the next, the carnage
of a Baghdad marketplace

The eternal victim's story
buried and waiting
by the side of the road

Meanwhile, an old Sufi—
prayer beads in one hand
and grain in the other—
sows wheat in the desert

Praying for all, praying for rain

*N.B.: I.E.D.s are "improvised explosive
devices" commonly used in the Iraq War*

## The Fierce Deities Are Clear

What will it take to really break through
the Himalayan pile of shit
that dams up the wild river that could be your life?
A casual glance?
Taking a stab at it now and then?
Practicing whenever you feel like it?
No, that just won't do.
It'll take a flaming, diamond sword
to rend the veils between you and the Holy One.
The Fierce Deities are clear on this:
"Open your heart now—or else forget about it!"

# Hard, Hard Work

Just another day at the old office—
dragging my sorry ass
over to the zendo
lighting the candles
ringing the bell
sitting in utter stillness
in the cool darkness
just before dawn
with five gorgeous women
all opening their hearts
in the vast, diamond silence
all radiating a hidden wholeness
shimmering with terror and bliss

Well, it's hard, hard work—
but hey, somebody's gotta do it

# Dakini Wisdom

Nine bows to you, my dear sisters!
If you meet the Buddha on the road,
or anywhere else for that matter,
and it's a man—cut his balls off!

And if he keeps on smiling—
then, just maybe, you can trust him.

*N.B.: A dakini is a fierce, erotic female angel
that appears to practitioners of Buddhist
Tantra to teach, inspire and admonish.*

# The Great Way

*after Dogen & Genpo*

To follow the way
Is to study the self

To study the self
Is to integrate the self

To integrate the self
Is to transcend the self

And transcending the self
Truly manifests the Great Way

# Voices from Hell

*a work-in-progress*

During a Zen sesshin, you sit for hours
facing a blank white wall, in silence.
Whenever you leave the present moment,
as you bring yourself back—
you note the voice that lured you away.
When Jesus exorcised the demons—
He called them by name.
I call mine: The Voices from Hell.

*There's something wrong with you.*
*You've never been good enough.*
*You should be in control at all times.*
*If you're not in total control,*
*you should be ashamed of yourself.*
*Be sure to finish all your work*
*before you go out and play.*
*You are what you do.*
*You can do better than that!*
*Be a good boy and they'll love you.*
*Be perfect and they'll adore you.*
*If you don't get paid, it isn't work—*
*it's a hobby.*
*The bottom line is still the bottom line.*

*The next moment is more important.*
*Preparing for a more important moment*
*is what this moment is all about.*
*You should know.*
*You should be able to please*
*all of the people, all of the time.*

*If you want it done right,*
*do it yourself.*
*If you're not in control, who are you?*
*Disguise that spare tire.*
*Avoid crowds, they're harder to control.*
*Nobody really gives a shit.*
*All you are is a cow—when the milk*
*dries up—you're hamburger!*
*If you're not the best, who are you?*
*Never, ever, be proven wrong.*
*Losing an argument is death itself.*
*Never let anyone else have the last word.*

*It's a dog eat dog world out there.*
*If you don't look out for #1—*
*you'll end up penniless,*
*living under the overpass,*
*with newspapers for blankets.*
*Bigger is better. Numbers matter.*
*It's all or nothing.*
*They could do better if they tried.*
*Every person, place or thing*
*was created by God—to be*
*judged by me.*
*In Control We Trust!*
*How unenlightened they all are.*
*Who does he think he is to judge me!*
*After all I've done for you,*
*this is the thanks I get?*
*Well, fuck you!*
*Let's see how you like my silence!*

*Money validates everything.*
*Never be late.*
*Responsible people worry—*
*hell, somebody's gotta do it!*
*Hide your terror with a smile.*
*Never show your anger.*
*You should be able to control*
*your emotions.*
*Keep it together.*
*Asking for help is for the weak.*
*Don't be too happy—you know*
*it won't last.*
*Life is just one problem after another.*
*No! That's wrong. You gotta work on this.*
*Practice makes perfect.*
*Time is money.*
*He should, she should, they should, it should.*
*I should be concerned about what others*
*might think of me.*
*The beatings will continue until morale improves.*

When I believe any of these voices,
or on the other hand,
when I struggle to rid myself of them—
I immediately descend into the depths of hell.
But when I can simply recognize the voices,
and just let them be—
they all, eventually, dissolve like clouds...
revealing blue sky, nothing but the vast blue sky.

# The Pearl of Great Price

The Pearl of Great Price for folks on the spiritual journey,
no matter what arises, is this simple, six word question:
"How do I practice with this?"
No matter what arises. No matter what arises.

## In Light of Merton

The true nature of our being
is a great spaciousness
which is untouched
by sin and illusion.
A truly vast openness
which is unstained
by the fantasies of our mind
or the brutalities of our will.

Merton called it *Le Point Vierge*
(The Virgin Point)

It's like a pure diamond—blazing
with the invisible light of heaven.
It's in everybody.
And if we could only unveil it
and live in light of it—
we would radiate a peace
that would make all the darkness
and all the cruelty vanish forever.

We practice to unveil it—
and to learn how to live in light of it.

# The Great Surprise

Won't it be the great surprise, when
we realize, with our own eyes, that
from the very beginning, nothing
was ever lacking.

# Index

## A

## B

## C

## D

## E

## F

## G

## H

# About the Author

Joe Zarantonello is a teacher, poet and the creator of The Integral Journal. Joe's undergraduate degree is from the University of Notre Dame where he majored in The Great Books. His M.A. is from University College (Dublin) where he studied the Irish poets.

Joe spends most of his time at home, with his wife Pam, running Loose Leaf Hollow — a guesthouse for solitary or guided retreats in the rolling knobs outside of Bardstown, Kentucky. He published his first book of poetry, Green Bamboo, in 2005.

This poem is framed and hangs on the wall beside the door at Loose Leaf Hollow—

## *My Passion*

My vocation
And my avocation
My work
And my play
Is helping others
Create a way
To unveil
The hidden brilliance

Respons͙
or request͙                    ͙ on Loose Leaf Hollow Retreats
can be sent ͙

͙ Zarantonello
1766 Barnes Road
Bardstown, KY 40004
502·348·0201
joe@looseleafhollow.com